100% UNOFFICIAL

100% UNOFFICIAL

100% UNOFFICIAL

100% UNOFFICIAL

100% UNOFFICIAL

100%
UNOFFICIAL

First published in Great Britain 2025 by 100% Unofficial, a part of Farshore
An imprint of HarperCollins*Publishers*
1 London Bridge Street, London SE1 9GF
www.farshore.co.uk

HarperCollins*Publishers*
Macken House, 39/40 Mayor Street Upper,
Dublin 1, D01 C9W8, Ireland

Written by Ben Wilson

ISBN 978 0 00 877307 6
Printed in Malaysia
001

A CIP catalogue record for this title is available from the British Library.

100% UNOFFICIAL

TAYLOR SWIFT

GUIDE: VOLUME 2

CONTENTS

08 FACT FILE

10 TAYLOR TIMELINE

12 ERAS TOUR WORLD MAP

14 ALBUM SPOTLIGHT: THE TORTURED POETS DEPARTMENT

16 13 ... TOP ERAS TOUR ACOUSTIC SONGS

18 TOTALLY TAYLOR: BEST ERAS TOUR MOMENTS

20 SWIFTIES' ACTIVITIES: YOUR SWIFTIE JOURNAL

22 13 ... BEST AWARDS

22 ALBUM SPOTLIGHT: FEARLESS (TV)

24 TOTALLY TAYLOR: SPREADING THE LOVE

26 13 ... BEST ERAS TOUR SURPRISE GUESTS

28 SWIFTIES' ACTIVITIES: THE BLANK SPACES QUIZ

30 ALBUM SPOTLIGHT: RED (TV)

32 13 ... BEST AWARDS

34 TOTALLY TAYLOR: EVERY ERA EXPLAINED

36 SWIFTIES' ACTIVITIES: DESIGN YOUR OWN '22' T-SHIRT

37 SWIFTIES' ACTIVITIES: REPUTATION SNAKE MAZE

38 ALBUM SPOTLIGHT: SPEAK NOW (TV)

40 TOTALLY TAYLOR: BEST DRESSED TOUR GOERS

42 13 ... BEST TAYLOR EASTER EGGS

44 SWIFTIES' ACTIVITIES: ERAS TOUR WORDSEARCH

45 SWIFTIES' ACTIVITIES: MAKE THE FRIENDSHIP BRACELETS

46 ALBUM SPOTLIGHT: 1989 (TV)

48 13 ... TOP ERAS TOUR SUPPORT ACTS

50 TOTALLY TAYLOR: ERAS TOUR FAN FRENZY

52 SWIFTIES' ACTIVITIES: WHICH TAYLOR ERA ARE YOU?

54 ALBUM SPOTLIGHT: TAYLOR SWIFT HOLIDAY COLLECTION

56 TOTALLY TAYLOR: FAMOUS SWIFTIES

58 13 ... BEST MUSIC VIDEOS

60 SWIFTIES' ACTIVITIES: THE ULTIMATE SWIFTIES' TRIVIA QUIZ

62 ALBUM SPOTLIGHT: TS12

64 13 ... VAULT TRACKS YOU NEED TO HEAR

66 TOTALLY TAYLOR: ERAS TOUR STATS

68 SWIFTIES' ACTIVITIES: CUTE COLOURING

69 ANSWERS

TAYLOR SWIFT FACT FILE

Everything you need to know about the Queen of Pop!

Taylor looking a million dollars at the 2025 Grammy Awards!

NAME:

Taylor Alison Swift

BIRTHDAY:

13 December 1989

STAR SIGN:

Sagittarius, which means she's curious and energetic. Also – and *Lover* fans will love this one – its symbol is **the archer**!

HEIGHT:

She's pretty tall at 1.80 m

BIRTHPLACE:

West Reading, Pennsylvania, USA

TV PICKS:

Taylor's cat **Meredith Grey** is named after a character from ***Grey's Anatomy***. Tay also loves *Gilmore Girls* and *Stranger Things*!

FAVE COLOUR:

Amazingly, it's not red or gold or even maroon. Taylor told Ellen DeGeneres that her **favourite colour is purple**!

FILM LOVES:

Love Actually, *The Martian*, *He's Just Not That Into You*, *Pan's Labyrinth* and *The Shape of Water* are some of Taylor's film faves!

BEST BOOKS:

Daphne du Maurier's novel *Rebecca* inspired the song **'tolerate it'**. Growing up, Tay also loved *Stargirl* by Jerry Spinelli, which is all about the power of individuality!

HOBBIES:
Tay loves baking, cooking, collecting antiques and making snow globes!

Tay has reinvented herself countless times – but never goes out of style!

ACTING:
TayTay voiced Andrey in *The Lorax* and has also appeared in *Cats*, *New Girl* and *CSI: Crime Scene Investigation*!

ANIMAL LOVER:
Her 3 cats are super famous now, too! They're called **Meredith Grey**, **Olivia Benson** and **Benjamin Button**.

INFLUENCES:
Tim McGraw, hence the song of the same name! Tay also adores Fleetwood Mac legend **Stevie Nicks**, **Joni Mitchell** and **The Chicks** – who guested on **'Soon You'll Get Better'**.

FOODIE FAVES:
Tay is known to be a massive foodie and she recently made Travis **cinnamon rolls** as a pre-game treat!

NUMBER:
You should know this one by now! It's **13 of course!** T-Swift was born on Friday 13th and her first album went gold in 13 weeks.

SPORTS:
She regularly supports boyfriend Travis Kelce at **NFL games**. Tay also enjoys watching bowling and hockey.

CHRISTMAS:
Taylor loves the holiday season so much that her friends joke she's an elf. In 2014, she sent treats to 32 fans around the world to say **Happy Swiftmas**!

TAYLOR TIMELINE

All the big dates from Tay's three-and-a-half decades on planet Earth!

1989

Taylor Alison Swift is **born on 13th December** in Reading, Pennsylvania, to Scott and Andrea. 3 years later she's joined by her brother, Austin!

Taylor with her parents at boyfriend Travis' Chiefs game.

2010

The epic ***Fearless* tour** enters its second year. Tay plays **118 shows** in total, bringing in more than $63 million! She follows this up with the release of ***Speak Now***, from which **'Mean' wins more Grammys** – for Best Country Song and Best Country Solo Performance!

1989 **2002** **2006** **2008** **2010** **2012**

2002

At just 11 years old, Taylor performs **'The Star Spangled Banner'** during a Philadelphia 76ers hockey match. A computer repair man shows her how to play 3 guitar chords – C, D and G – and she **writes her first song**. It's called **'Lucky You'**!

2006

The real rise to fame begins. Taylor's first single, **'Tim McGraw'**, bursts onto the USA's **Billboard music chart** and stays there for 8 months. It's followed up by **debut album *Taylor Swift***, which spends 24 weeks on top of the **country chart**!

2008

Big summer single **'Love Story'** turns Taylor into a worldwide household name, ahead of the release of album number 2. ***Fearless*** lands in November and goes on to win **Album of the Year** at the Grammy Awards.

This 'Love Story' dress from the *Fearless* tour was perfect!

2012

Keeping to her every-2-years schedule, Tay unleashes spectacular fourth album ***Red***. Its big singles include **'We Are Never Ever Getting Back Together'** and **'I Knew You Were Trouble'**. However, hardcore fans agree that **'All Too Well'** is the best thing she's ever done!

Tay celebrated her 30th birthday performing at the Jingle Ball in New York, 2019.

2014

For album 5, Taylor goes full-on pop! ***1989*** is named after her birth year. Its lead single **'Shake It Off'** becomes a pop culture phenomenon. She celebrates **turning 25** with a massive **New York party** alongside the Haim sisters, Jay-Z and Beyoncé!

2019

Pop is the theme again for album number 7. Taylor is head over heels for British beau Joe Alwyn and that's reflected in songs like **'London Boy'** and **'I Think He Knows'** on ***Lover***. **'Cruel Summer'** is the fan favourite, but it won't be **number 1** until 2023!

2024

After wowing America throughout 2023, year 2 of The Eras Tour sees 11th album ***The Tortured Poets Department*** incorporated into the set. It finishes up as the **most popular tour of any artist** in history and spawns its own **movie and book**!

2014 2017 2019 2020 2022 2024 2025

2017

Taylor takes an extra year to make sixth album ***Reputation***. With good reason: it's become popular to **criticise her in the media** and the record is a **fightback against those who've tried to bring her down**. Its **snake symbol** remains iconic to this day!

2020

T-Swift brings the world some joy during a scary pandemic, by releasing **2 albums in just 5 months**! Both ***folklore*** and ***evermore*** strip back her usually grand arrangements and usher in a new, more grown-up era for our girl.

2022

"It's me, hi …" Those 3 words become a meme across social media as lead single **'Anti-Hero'** ushers in the ***Midnights*** era. In November, Taylor announces **The Eras Tour**, during which she'll play 44 songs over three-and-a-half hours. Fans are so keen that the **ticketing system crashes**!

2025

Taylor is now, by some margin, the **biggest superstar in the world**. *TTPD* goes winless at the Grammys, but she still **thanks her fans** on X after the show. "We couldn't be prouder of what this album has accomplished," Tay writes. "Until our next board meeting."

ERAS TOUR WORLD MAP

These are all the venues Taylor played on the greatest tour in music history!

Key

- Canada
- North America
- South America
- UK
- Europe
- Asia
- Australia

Toronto – Nov 2024

Vancouver – Nov 2024
The Eras Tour **came to a close** in the beautiful Canadian city of Vancouver. Fans were so desperate to attend, that **last-minute ticket prices skyrocketed** up to $15,000!

Los Angeles – Aug 2023
TayTay played **6 dates in LA**, the most of any American city. She was joined by trio of sisters group **Haim** each night for a noisy rendition of **'no body, no crime'**.

Las Vegas – Mar 2023

Arlington – Mar/Apr 2023

Houston – Apr 2023

Atlanta – Apr 2023

Nashville – May 2023

Philadelphia – May 2023

Foxborough – May 2023

East Rutherford – May 2023

Glendale – Mar 2023
The Eras Tour **kicked off** in the 78,600-capacity State Farm Stadium. **'Tim McGraw'** and **'mirrorball'** were the surprise songs, as fans worldwide gushed in awe.

State Farm Stadium is home to NFL team the Arizona Cardinals!

Chicago – Jun 2023

Detroit – Jun 2023

Pittsburgh – Jun 2023

Minneapolis – Jun 2023

Cincinnati – Jun/Jul 2023

Kansas City – Jul 2023

Denver – Jul 2023

Seattle – Jul 2023

Santa Clara – Jul 2023

Tampa – Apr 2023
Tampa saw Taylor perform for the first time since her split from Joe Alwyn was announced. No wonder she chose **'You're On Your Own, Kid'** as a surprise song on night 2!

Miami – Oct 2024

New Orleans – Oct 2024

Indianapolis – Nov 2024

Mexico City – Aug 2023

Buenos Aires – Nov 2023

Rio de Janeiro – Nov 2023

São Paulo – Nov 2023

Edinburgh – Jun 2024

Liverpool – Jun 2024

Cardiff – Jun 2024

Dublin – Jun 2024

London – Jun/Aug 2024
The English capital got **more dates than anywhere else** in the world, with 8 shows. **Ed Sheeran** was a guest star – and obviously Tay had to say goodbye with **'So Long, London'**!

Warsaw – Aug 2024
There was sad news following the 3 Warsaw shows, as Tay had to **cancel her Vienna concerts due to a security threat**. They ended up being the only dates across the entire tour that didn't happen.

Wembley Stadium lit up the night sky when Taylor played her 8 gigs there!

Paris – May 2024
It was all change in Paris, as Taylor **added 7 songs** from *The Tortured Poets Department* to the set! But it did mean she bid farewell to **'tolerate it'** and **'The Archer'** to make room.

Stockholm – May 2024

Lisbon – May 2024

Madrid – May 2024

Lyon – Jun 2024

Amsterdam – Jul 2024

Zürich – Jul 2024

Milan – Jul 2024

Gelsenkirchen – Jul 2024

Hamburg – Jul 2024

Munich – Jul 2024

Taylor smashed records in the Melbourne sunlight!

Tokyo – Feb 2024

Sydney – Feb 2024

Singapore – Mar 2024

Melbourne – Feb 2024
Tay is always breaking records wherever she goes! In Melbourne, she pulled in **288,000 fans across 3 days – more than any other act** who has ever played in the city!

ALBUM SPOTLIGHT

THE TORTURED POETS DEPARTMENT

DOUBLE THE FUN

Taylor announced her 11th album, *The Tortured Poets Department* (or *TTPD*), at the 2024 Grammy Awards. But that was just the beginning of the journey! Just 2 hours after its release in April that year, the album was expanded with *The Anthology* – a second set of 15 additional songs. Naturally, they were all amazing!

Florence and Taylor wowed Wembley with their 'Florida!!!' duet.

BONUS BONANZA

4 different versions of *TTPD* were released on CD, each with a unique **bonus track**: **'The Manuscript'**, **'The Bolter'**, **'The Albatross'** and **'The Black Dog'**. Then, when *The Anthology* came out on vinyl, we got more bonuses: awesome acoustic versions of **'Fortnight'**, **'Down Bad'**, **'But Daddy I Love Him'** and **'Guilty as Sin?'**!

QUEEN OF MY CHART

In the first week after release, Taylor held the top **14 places on the US Billboard Top 100** – the first time this had ever been done! **'Fortnight'** took top spot, followed by **'Down Bad'** and **'I Can Do It With A Broken Heart'**.

SPOTIFY SMASH

TTPD obliterated loads of records. Of course it did! It was the seventh Taylor album in a row to **sell a million copies in its first week**. It topped the USA music charts for 17 weeks and got the **most Spotify streams ever** – for both a single day and a single week!

ONE FOR THE LADIES

'Clara Bow' is named after a famous **silent film actor**, and the lyrics are about girl power. The song also mentions legendary Fleetwood Mac singer **Stevie Nicks**. "Clara Bow was the first 'it girl'," Taylor told *Variety*. "[And] Stevie Nicks is an icon and an **incredible example** for anyone who wants to write songs and make music."

FLO RIDIN'

Post Malone guested on **'Fortnight'**, while **Florence + The Machine** teamed up with Tay on **'Florida!!!'**. And not just for the album. During Taylor's final Eras Tour date in London, Florence appeared on stage for a **surprise performance** of that song. Fans were completely blown away!

PRIZE PUB

The Anthology brought unexpected fame to a small pub in South London! **The Black Dog was inundated with Taylor fans** for months, thanks to the song of the same name. The owners hosted singalongs, and the pub's events manager Lily Bottomley said the reaction was "crazy"!

HAIL TO THE CHIEF

Lots of the songs on *TTPD* were highly likely about Taylor's break-ups with Joe Alwyn and Matty Healy. But new beau **Travis Kelce**, an NFL player for the Kansas City Chiefs, was clearly referenced in fantastic *The Anthology* track **'So High School'**. It became an instant fan fave, and was brilliantly mixed with **'But Daddy I Love Him'** on The Eras Tour!

The name for *The Tortured Poets Department* was apparently inspired by a WhatsApp group containing Joe Alwyn and 2 of his friends. It was called 'The Tortured Man Club'!

13 ... TOP ERAS TOUR ACOUSTIC SONGS

Every single night of The Eras Tour, Taylor played a minimum of 2 surprise songs on either guitar or piano. These were the highlights!

1 MIRRORBALL

"I was trying to think of sort of an eloquent way to say that I love you … and I came up with **'I'm a mirrorball'**." Those were Taylor's words as she launched into the **first ever surprise song**, in Arizona. We love you too, Taylor!

2 LONDON BOY

Despite splitting from Joe Alwyn, Taylor was always going to play the song she wrote about him in his hometown. The only surprise is it took until her **fifth Wembley gig** to do so!

3 US / OUT OF THE WOODS

Taylor and **Gracie Abrams** were nominated for Best Pop Duo/Group Performance at the Grammy Awards 2025. So, in Toronto, **the pair teamed up to play 'Us' acoustically** – and mixed in **'Out Of The Woods'** to make it truly unforgettable!

4 YOU'RE LOSING ME

Melbourne residents were among the luckiest Eras Tour goers. They got to hear **'You're Losing Me'**, a fan favourite from the ***Late Night Edition of Midnights***, live for the first time ever!

5 YOU ARE IN LOVE

Many fans reckon this is Taylor's **most touching ballad** and she unleashed a breathtaking rendition – growing visibly **emotional** towards the end – on night 2 in Los Angeles. You can see it for yourself as part of ***The Eras Tour* movie**.

6 BETTER MAN

Foxborough fans were treated to something truly unexpected here. **'Better Man'** was originally gifted to country band **Little Big Town**, before Tay recorded it herself for ***Red (Taylor's Version)***. Hearing it live cemented its place in her catalogue.

Country band Little Big Town have been making catchy tunes since 1998. They've released 11 albums, and 'Better Man' went to number 1 on the US Country chart!

7 BACK TO DECEMBER

A true Taylor tearjerker came to life in Denver. Fans' **light-up wristbands turned from blue to purple** as they swayed along to this absolute classic from ***Speak Now***.

8 I WISH YOU WOULD

One of the most **underrated tracks** of Taylor's entire career got a wonderful airing in Chicago. Taylor belted the ***1989*** banger out during her acoustic set, while 50,000 fans sang along to her every word. **It's all good!**

9 EXILE

Wow, wow, wow. Bon Iver frontman **Justin Vernon** originally guested on this ***folklore*** epic, but he wasn't there live to perform it. Instead, the **Los Angeles crowd chanted his words** perfectly. Listen on YouTube and feel the goosebumps.

10 DEATH BY A THOUSAND CUTS / GETAWAY CAR

For her very **last night in London**, Tay brought out longtime collaborator **Jack Antonoff** – and the pair absolutely nailed this mash-up of 2 signature tunes, with **both playing acoustic guitars.**

As well as co-writing smash hits, Jack Antonoff is one of Tay's closest friends. He's also in the band Fun and Bleachers.

11 MARY'S SONG / SO HIGH SCHOOL / EVERYTHING HAS CHANGED

The second year of The Eras Tour saw **'So High School'** become a setlist regular – meaning Amsterdam fans were even more surprised when it reappeared in this mash-up! **Travis Kelce** was watching live and it was clear that Tay **aimed all 3 songs at him**.

12 CALL IT WHAT YOU WANT

The Taylor fanbase adores this track, as its one of the most powerful on ***Reputation*** – and all **about her disappearing when the media turned on her** following *1989*. Hearing it stripped down on piano in Cincinnati brought many fans to tears.

13 LONG LIVE / NEW YEAR'S DAY / THE MANUSCRIPT

The last mash-up of the tour took place in Vancouver. Taylor blended her final *Reputation* song, **'New Year's Day'**, and her **most recent song** of the time, **'The Manuscript'** from *The Tortured Poets Department* – then tied them together with the spectacular **'Long Live'** from *Speak Now*!

TOTALLY TAYLOR: BEST ERAS TOUR MOMENTS

How do you pick 7 highlights from a 45-song set? It's basically impossible, but let's give it a try, anyway ...

MISS AMERICANA & THE HEARTBREAK PRINCE

Many Swifties proclaim the **opening track of The Eras Tour** to be the greatest moment of their life. Taylor snuck onstage beneath a **wave of pink clamshells** held by her dancers, before launching into this *Lover* favourite. If you were there, you've probably got **goosebumps** just reading this!

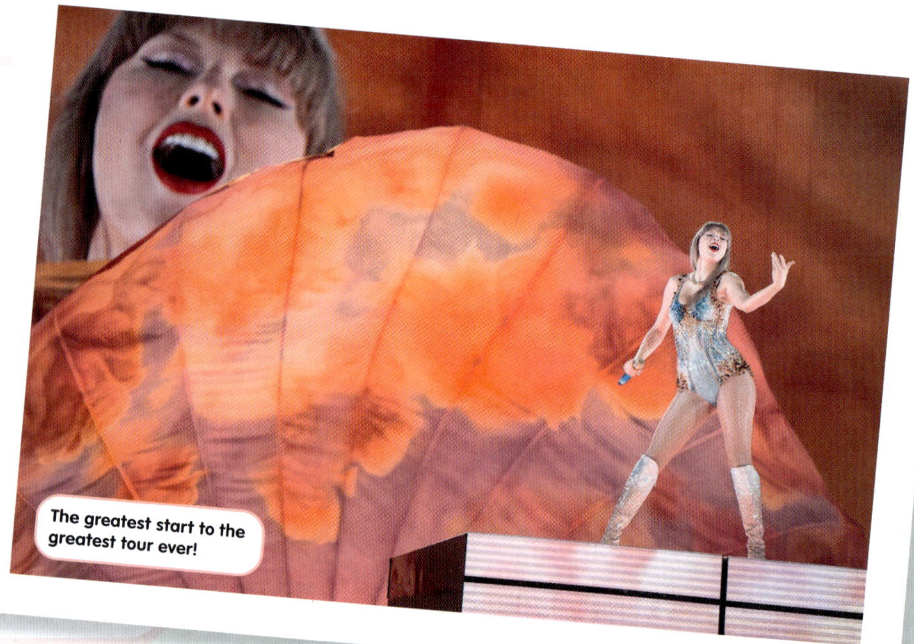

The greatest start to the greatest tour ever!

Other *1989* favourites included 'Blank Space' and 'Shake It Off'.

STYLE

While this *1989* single has always been considered a **Taylor signature**, it reached epic scale on The Eras Tour. Fans were given **wristbands** on entry at each stadium, and these **flashed like crazy** as she nailed the last half of the song – creating an incredible visual spectacle!

BETTY

A magic moment was Taylor performing songs from *folklore* with her set made to look like a **cabin in the woods**. Favourite songs **'the 1'** and **'the last great american dynasty'** both shone – but beautiful acoustic number **'betty'** stole this section of the show.

Taylor owned the stage in her blazer during 'The Man'.

THE MAN

TayTay's **empowering lady anthem** took on an even bigger lease of life during The Eras Tour. She performed it in a **sparkly blazer and thigh-high boots**, oozing **female boss energy** as fans lapped up every second!

'Karma' was one of 7 *Midnights* favourites each night – and the final song!

CRUEL SUMMER

Swifties feared they'd never hear this live when the **Lover Fest tour was cancelled** in 2020. They needn't have worried. Not only did it get **everyone out of their seats** 2 songs into the show, but videos of fans **shouting and screaming** its incredible bridge remained a TikTok phenomenon from the first show to the last!

KARMA

The final track of each night made for the **perfect farewell**. Taylor unleashed this favourite from *Midnights*, thanked her band, backing singers, dancers and crew, then sent everyone home happy with a **spectacular fireworks show**. She even **changed the lyrics** for Travis Kelce!

Don't call her kid, don't her baby ... Taylor really showed us her colours! Which *folklore* dress was your fave?

ILLICIT AFFAIRS

Taylor only performed the **end section** of this *folklore* fave, but its treatment was completely different from the recorded version – and so, so good. **Falling to her knees** to belt out its despairing lyrics led to fans rechristening it **'illicit affairs (angry version)'**!

SWIFTIES' ACTIVITIES

YOUR SWIFTIE JOURNAL

Taylor is all about her fans. She has millions, but every single one is unique! To celebrate that, here's the chance to big up your own personal love for Taylor. Make sure you fill in your favourite songs, albums and Eras Tour moments, then enjoy looking back on them in the years to come!

Making sparkly memories at Wembley, London!

NAME:

AGE:

WHERE I LIVE:

TOP 5 TAYLOR SONGS:

1.
2.
3.
4.
5.

TOP 3 TAYLOR ALBUMS:

1.
2.
3.

FAVOURITE LYRICS:

Big love for Taylor – these lucky fans got to the front!

FAVE PIECE OF TAYLOR MERCH:

FAVOURITE TAYLOR CAT:

WHAT I'D MAKE TAYLOR FOR DINNER:

WHAT I'D SAY IF I EVER MET TAYLOR:

BEST ERAS TOUR PERFORMANCE:

BEST ERAS TOUR MOMENT:

TAYLOR ALBUMS OWNED:

ALBUM SPOTLIGHT

FEARLESS (TAYLOR'S VERSION)

COMEBACK QUEEN

In 2019, Taylor's record company sold off the rights to her first 6 albums. So, she decided to re-record them all herself – and throw in several unheard tracks from the Vault, written at the same time as each album, into the mix too! *Fearless (Taylor's Version)* was the first re-recorded album to be released, in April 2021.

Taylor won Best Country Female Artist at the 2008 AMAs!

FAIRYTALE KISS

The new additions from the Vault included **'Today Was A Fairytale'**. This song was originally released as part of the soundtrack to the 2010 film ***Valentine's Day***, in which Taylor played student Felicia Miller. She got to kiss **Taylor Lautner**, sparking a brief real-life relationship!

URBAN LEGEND

Country favourite **Keith Urban's appearance** on Vault track **'That's When'** was more than a decade in the making. **Taylor was the opening act** on Keith's *Escape Together* world tour, **way back in 2009**!

ROMEO RETURN

Unsurprisingly, the classic **'Love Story'** was chosen as the first single from *Fearless (Taylor's Version)*. It went straight to **number 1** on the **US Hot Country Songs chart**, soon joined by **'You All Over Me'** and **'Mr Perfectly Fine'**.

ORIGINAL FLAVOURS

To stay true to the original record, Taylor **brought back most of the musicians who worked with her** when it was first released in 2008. Folk-pop star **Colbie Caillat** also flew into Nashville especially to meet Taylor and re-record her vocals for **'Breathe'**.

HELLO, BYE BYE

Fans were especially happy to get an official release of final Vault track **'Bye Bye Baby'**. The song is about **letting go of a broken relationship** – and a **demo version** of it had been shared by committed fans over the internet for more than a decade!

FLYING SOLO

Fearless (Taylor's Version) features **26 tracks** overall, 11 of which Taylor **wrote herself**. The self-penned songs include **'Fifteen'**, **'Love Story'**, **'Change'** and Vault track **'Mr Perfectly Fine'**.

FAMOUS FRIENDS

Olivia Rodrigo and **Conan Gray** were drafted in to help promote the album. A TikTok video showed them leaping about on a bed to **'You Belong With Me'**, while Instagram users saw them goofing around to **'White Horse'**!

The release of the original *Fearless* album saw Taylor bring a sparkle to every performance – even when it came to her guitars!

TOTALLY TAYLOR: SPREADING THE LOVE

T-Swift is famed for her generosity and philanthropy. Zooming round the planet on The Eras Tour didn't change that! These were some of her acts of kindness ...

Taylor is known to be super welcoming to fans at signings, always offering hugs and selfies!

CHRISTMAS TREATS

The Eras Tour shut down briefly for a Christmas break in 2023, but that didn't prevent Taylor from spreading some joy. **She gave $250,000 to Operation Breakthrough**, an education centre in Kansas City. "Thank you, @taylorswift13, for making our holiday season shine even brighter!" they wrote on X.

Hurricane Helene sadly decimated Florida in September 2024.

HURRICANE CLEAN-UP

Hurricane Helene wreaked havoc across Florida just months after Taylor had wowed local fans in Tampa. In response to the natural disaster, **Tay donated a colossal $5 million to relief efforts**.

STAR GIRL

When 7-year-old Bella Lanzino arrived at The Eras Tour in Las Vegas, her mum **gave a letter to an usher to be passed on to Taylor**. Incredibly, halfway through the show it was returned to her – and **Taylor had signed it**!

LUCKY TRUCKERS

Taylor really **looks after her crew** on all her tours. As the first year of The Eras Tour came to a close, it emerged that **she'd given $100,000 to each of her truck drivers**. With around 50 drivers on the tour, that's a **total of $5 million**!

Taylor belting out 'The Man' on The Eras Tour.

CREW LOVE

Once The Eras Tour was over, **Taylor dished out another round of bonuses** to everyone involved. That includes lighting technicians, instrument techs, hair and makeup artists, and so many more. Overall, she gave her team and crew **$197 million**!

UK FOOD BANKS ...

While on the UK leg of the tour, Taylor made a "generous donation" to **1,400 food banks and community organisations** in Edinburgh, Liverpool, Cardiff and London. Sophie Carre of The Trussell Trust, who run the food banks, said, "we weren't expecting it, but obviously we were **really delighted** when we found out".

... AND USA ONES, TOO

Food banks in the USA got help from Taylor, too. At the very start of the tour, she made **donations in Glendale and Las Vegas**. "We don't know about you, but we're **feeling grateful** on this day, March 22!" wrote Nevada's Three Square organisation, on Instagram.

Food banks give essentials to families across the globe.

13 ... BEST ERAS TOUR SURPRISE GUESTS

No Taylor gig is ever predictable. She always loves to surprise the crowd with a special guest or 2 – were you there to catch any of these megastars?

1 MARCUS MUMFORD

Mumford & Sons' lead singer was the very **first surprise guest** on The Eras Tour. He joined Taylor to sing **'cowboy like me'** in Las Vegas, in March 2023 – setting a trend that would last nearly 2 years!

Marcus Mumford actually featured on 'cowboy like me' from *evermore*. Listen closely!

2 HAIM

You'll see this **trio of sisters** popping up pretty regularly in this book, with good reason. Este, Danielle and Alana are great mates with Taylor – and they're brilliant! Taylor and Haim unleashed a perfect collab of **'no body, no crime'** during all 6 of her shows in Los Angeles.

3 PHOEBE BRIDGERS

Phoebe's **rise to global fame** coincided with her nights supporting Taylor on The Eras Tour. She wasn't only on board as an **opening act**, though: she also performed **'Nothing New'** with TayTay in Pennsylvania, Massachusetts and New Jersey.

4 AARON DESSNER

The National guitarist has **co-produced** Taylor's recent albums and became a semi-regular guest star on The Eras Tour as well. He sang **'The Great War'** with her in Tampa, **'ivy'** in Cincinnati and **'Would've Could've Should've'** in a spectacularly rainy show in Nashville!

5 JACK ANTONOFF

Taylor's other **long-time collaborator** made his first surprise appearance in New Jersey, where the pair belted out **'Getaway Car'** together. They went one better at Wembley, mashing up that favourite song with **'Death By A Thousand Cuts'** as 90,000 fans went crazy!

6 ICE SPICE

In May 2023, Taylor announced the **remix of 'Karma'** from *Midnights*, featuring new vocals from up-and-coming rapper Ice Spice – but that was only the first half of the surprise. The same day, **Ice Spice appeared onstage in New Jersey to perform the track live with Taylor** and was back for the next 2 nights.

7

MAREN MORRIS

Country star Maren stunned fans in Chicago by popping up onstage to perform **'You All Over Me'** with TayTay. The song originally appeared as a **Vault track** on *Fearless (Taylor's Version)*.

8

GRACIE ABRAMS

As well as being a regular **support act**, Gracie clocked up 4 Eras Tour appearances on stage with T-Swift. One of the highlights came in Toronto, while they unforgettably blended beautiful Gracie song **'Us'** with the always awesome **'Out Of The Woods'**!

9

ED SHEERAN

The **long-time friends** were reunited again on night 4 in London. Ed joined Taylor onstage for a **triple song mash-up** lasting more than 9 minutes. It covered **'Endgame'**, **'Everything Has Changed'** – and his own song **'Thinking Out Loud'**!

Taylor first met Hayley Williams at a Grammy Awards party back in 2009!

10

SABRINA CARPENTER

2024 was a supermassive year for Sabrina, and it got underway with her joining Taylor at the now-famous **Eras Tour piano**. The duo delivered a word-perfect **mash-up of 'White Horse'** and **'coney island'** together. Please please please can they collab again?

11

HAYLEY WILLIAMS

Paramore electrified crowds in support of Taylor, but those in attendance during night 2 at Wembley scored an additional treat. Front-person Hayley returned to the stage to perform **'Castles Crumbling'** with Tay – a song they performed on ***Speak Now (Taylor's Version)***.

12

FLORENCE WELCH

Just when everyone got to know the *TTPD* section of the Tour off by heart, Taylor stunned the entire universe on her **final night in London**. She unexpectedly burst into a one-off performance of **'Florida!!!'** – and was joined by the queen of **Florence & The Machine**!

Taylor and Travis celebrating the Kansas City chiefs winning the AFC Championship in January 2025.

13

TRAVIS KELCE

No, those words are not a misprint! Taylor's boyfriend didn't sing on The Eras Tour – but he did make for the most shocking **surprise guest** of all, appearing onstage in full tuxedo during a performance of **'I Can Do It With A Broken Heart'** at Wembley!

SWIFTIES' ACTIVITIES

THE BLANK SPACES QUIZ

How well do you know your idol? Test your knowledge with this brain-scratching blank spaces quiz!

1 What is the very first track on the very first Taylor Swift album?

2 What kind of farm did Taylor grow up on?

3 What is the name of Taylor's second album?

4 Which month does Taylor want to go back to on a classic track from *Speak Now*?

5 Name either of the 2 actors that starred in the music video for 'All Too Well (10 Minute Version)'.

6 What is both Taylor's year of birth and the title of her fifth album?

7 What animal does everyone associate with sixth album *Reputation*?

8 What's the first name of the Panic! At The Disco singer who joined TayTay on 'ME!'?

It's Mr Panic! At The Disco – but what's his real name?

9 **The second track on *Lover* gradually became a pop culture phenomenon. What's it called?**

10 **In which European city did Taylor perform the one-off *City of Lover* show?**

11 **What track from *folklore* features Justin Vernon from Bon Iver?**

12 **Which song from *evermore* is a tribute to Taylor's opera-singing grandma?**

13 **Name one of the sisters from Haim, the group that appears on 'no body, no crime'?**

14 **What colour is the haze Taylor sings about to kick off tenth album *Midnights*?**

15 **Which famous city does T-Swift sadly say "so long" to on *The Tortured Poets Department*?**

How did you do?

0–2: It's OK! You've got some blank spaces in your knowledge to fill, but you're still a super Swiftie.

3–6: A decent start. Read this book cover to cover and you'll be a mastermind in no time!

7–10: Who's afraid of little old you? Every quiz show host in the land, as you're on the verge of being a TayTay expert!

11–14: Incredible! You're definitely one of the most committed Swifties on the planet and knew every word on The Eras Tour!

15: Ummmm, Taylor, is that you? Get 'Cruel Summer' on at maximum volume, because you really do know everything there is to know about our girl!

ALBUM SPOTLIGHT

RED (TAYLOR'S VERSION)

A DIFFERENT SHADE

The second *Taylor's Version* (or *TV*) in the grand re-recording project landed in November 2021. We got 30 perfect tracks in total, including the 10-minute version of 'All Too Well' – which many fans consider the greatest moment of her glittering career.

Tay performing tracks from *Red* back in 2012.

WELL-LOVED

Taylor had teased an extended version of **'All Too Well'** since the original version landed in 2012. The 10-minute epic got a **short film directed by Taylor** herself! It starred **Sadie Sink** and **Dylan O'Brien**, and became the **longest number 1** (in terms of time) in the history of the US Billboard Top 100!

BOTTLED UP

Vault track **'Message In A Bottle'** was the first song Taylor co-wrote with Swedish music guru **Max Martin**. The pair then worked together on **'I Knew You Were Trouble', '22'** and **'We Are Never Ever Getting Back Together'** – but while those tracks made the original album, we had to wait until *Red (Taylor's Version)* to enjoy that very first collab!

FEELING 26

Red (Taylor's Version) **broke the female record for new entries in a single week** on the American charts. **26 songs** from the album burst into the **Top 100**, including **'All Too Well'** at number 1 and **'State of Grace'** at number 18.

HEAL CLOSE

"Musically and lyrically, *Red* resembled a heartbroken person," Swift wrote in a note to fans on Insta. The colour of the album was chosen to represent the emotions Taylor was experiencing during a difficult breakup.

GLOBE HUNTING

The official *Red (Taylor's Version)* **snow globe** is one of the rarest items of Taylor merch in existence. It features a tree with moving red leaves – and **sells for between £650 and £750!**

REMEMBERING RONAN

'Ronan' is the most upsetting song on *Red (Taylor's Version)*. It was written about **Ronan Thompson**, a little boy who died aged just 3 years old. Taylor had followed his mum **Maya's blog entries** about him. The song was released as a single in 2011, with **all proceeds going to cancer charities.**

NO SCARFING MATTER

The biggest mystery surrounding **'All Too Well'** remains the **scarf at the centre of the story**. It's said to be an elegant Gucci scarf that **Tay left at Maggie Gyllenhaal's house** when she was dating her brother **Jake** – the subject of the song. Maggie says she has no idea where it is now!

The original *Red* era marked one of Tay's more straightforward style choices, based on a certain colour. Naturally, she always looked fabulous!

13 ... BEST AWARDS

Taylor has amassed a colossal collection of trophies over the years. These are just a few of her biggest accolades ...

1 CMT MUSIC AWARDS BREAKTHROUGH VIDEO OF THE YEAR

Did you know that the first song to earn Taylor a trophy was **'Tim McGraw'**? The CMT Awards (or **Country Music Television Awards**) crowned her with Breakthrough Video of the Year in **2007**.

Tay looked spectacular at the MTV Video Music Awards in 2014, where she performed 'Shake It Off'.

2 MTV VIDEO OF THE YEAR

Tay has hoovered up this prize **5 times**! She got it for **'Bad Blood'** (2015), **'You Need To Calm Down'** (2019), **'All Too Well: The Short Film'** (2022), **'Anti-Hero'** (2023) and **'Fortnight'** (2024).

3 HIGHEST-GROSSING MUSIC TOUR

The Eras Tour is the most successful by any artist, ever – and that record is unlikely to be broken anytime soon. An estimated **10.1 million people** attended, making a grand total of **$2.07 billion**!

4 ALBUM OF THE YEAR

Taylor is the **only artist** in history to have **won the Grammy for Album of the Year 4 different times**! She claimed it for ***Fearless*** in 2010, ***1989*** in 2016, ***folklore*** in 2021 and ***Midnights*** in 2024.

5 TAYLOR SWIFT AWARD

Yes, she's even received an award **named after herself**! It was from **Broadcast Music, Inc** in 2016. "If they had chosen someone else to give the Taylor Swift Award to, I'd be kind of bummed about it," she joked as she collected the prize.

6 PERSON OF THE YEAR

Few awards on the planet are as cool as ***Time* magazine's Person Of The Year**. Past winners include philanthropist Greta Thunberg and US president Barack Obama. **Taylor earned this amazing award in 2023!**

7 TOP BILLBOARD 200 ALBUM

The Tortured Poets Department lost out to **Beyoncé** when it came to the 2025 Album of the Year Grammy, but there was some consolation when *TTPD* claimed the **Top Billboard 200 Album** accolade. *1989 (Taylor's Version)* was also nominated.

8 AMERICAN MUSIC AWARDS

Tay has been nominated for **49 AMAs** – and **won 40** of them! That puts her well ahead of music icon Whitney Houston, who collected 22. Amazing work!

9 GUINNESS WORLD RECORDS

Tay has clocked a mind-blowing **118 world records** over her magical career! Among them are **Most Streamed Female Act** on Spotify and **Fastest Selling Vinyl Album**, which was for *Midnights*.

10 ENTERTAINER OF THE YEAR

Taylor picked up this accolade from the **Country Music Association** when she was just 19 years old. It made her the **youngest winner ever!**

11 GLOBAL ICON AWARD

The **Brit Awards** are the biggest event on the UK music calendar and they commemorated Taylor's brilliance in 2021 with a **newly created Global Icon Award**. Kylie Minogue is the only other artist to receive the honour!

12 ONE NIGHT, FOUR GRAMMYS

Our girl cleaned up at the **Grammy Awards** in 2010. *Fearless* won **Album of the Year** and **Best Country Album**, while **'White Horse'** claimed **Best Female Country Vocal Performance** and **Best Country Song**!

T-Swift celebrating with all 4 of her Grammy Awards in 2010. What a win!

13 WOMAN OF THE DECADE

So much for worrying about her **reputation**: **Billboard** ended the 2010s by crowning Taylor the Woman of the Decade! During that period she **released 5 albums** and became the **planet's biggest pop star**. And she's got even better since then!

TOTALLY TAYLOR: EVERY ERA EXPLAINED

Not quite sure how to tell your *folklore* from your *evermore*, or *Speak Now* from *TTPD*? All is revealed here ...

TAYLOR SWIFT

Taylor's **big curls** made her early days memorable – and she was an immediate fashion icon, too. **Flowing dresses, cowboy boots and sunglasses** all throw back to Tay's **debut era**.

FEARLESS

The dresses remained flowing as Tay rose up the charts, but with a touch **more gold and a lot more sparkle**. She teased a grown-up fringe at times, and **ballgowns** became a popular look on the back of **'Love Story'**.

The cameras loved Taylor from the earliest days of her career!

T-Swift came to London to promote *Red* in 2012. She certainly dressed the part!

All *Speak Now* outfits must be the colour purple – including the album cover for *Taylor's Version*!

SPEAK NOW

This era is all about the colour purple. Taylor wore it on the album cover, performed in it regularly and even adopted it for the bottle colour of her first perfume, *Wonderstruck* – named after the lyrics to **'Enchanted'**.

RED

The colour speaks for itself, but it brought about another subtle style change too. Tay began to sport **sophisticated bangs**, wear **red lipstick**, high-waisted **shorts**, and **vintage dresses**. Our girl had officially grown up!

The *1989* Tour included 'Welcome To New York' and 'I Wish You Would'!

1989

'80s pop was the theme of the album named after **TayTay's birth year**, and she styled herself accordingly. Her hair became a **blonde bob**, while outfits included **sequinned jumpsuits, crop tops and skater skirts**.

REPUTATION

An extended **break from the limelight** inspired Tay to turn **rebel** when she returned with *Reputation*. **Black catsuits, leather, dark lipstick and snake imagery** keep this era popular with fans nearly a decade later.

Loved-up Taylor added a whole new flood of colour to her wardrobe!

LOVER

The follow-up to *Reputation* was like **going from night to day**! Tay had fallen in love with British actor Joe Alwyn, and her style reflected this new lease of life. **Pastel colours** dominated her wardrobe, accompanied by images of **lollipops, butterflies and rainbows**!

FOLKLORE & EVERMORE

Taylor stripped everything back for her **sister albums**, released while the world was in lockdown. Her folksy outlook turned into **cottagecore** visuals, with **braided hair, cosy cardigans and plaid shirts**. The lumberjack look suited her, so much!

MIDNIGHTS

Not many stars can pull off a flawless **'70s makeover** – but naturally, T-Swift breezed it! **Sweater vests and corduroys** were a feature of photo shoots, while performances went big on **sequin dresses and faux fur**.

THE TORTURED POETS DEPARTMENT

Taylor showcased herself as the **queen of reinvention** once again with album 11. **Inspired by style icons** such as Versace and Vivienne Westwood, she wowed on stage and in real life with **bustiers, corsets and Oxford heels**.

DESIGN YOUR OWN '22' T-SHIRT

Taylor's '22' T-shirt has become iconic. Now you can make your own!

Back in 2012, Taylor wore a white T-shirt in the video for **'22'** with a simple slogan: **"Not a lot going on at the moment."** The Eras Tour saw her bring it back to perform that song – but with **something different written on it every night**! It became one of the tour's copycat trends, with fans turning up to concerts in their own customised versions. **What will your slogan say?**

TOP TAY TIPS ...

Keep your slogan to somewhere between 5–10 words.

Try it out on a piece of paper before drawing in the book.

Pick out 2 or 3 words to write in red. Write the rest in black pen!

REPUTATION SNAKE MAZE

Can you make it through the maze to be reunited with Taylor's legendary snake from *Reputation*?

SPEAK NOW (TAYLOR'S VERSION)

BETTER THAN REVENGE

Fans who attended The Eras Tour in Nashville got a special treat: the announcement of Taylor's third re-recorded album! It was released in July 2023, with 22 tracks in total. Fall Out Boy and Paramore's Hayley Williams were among the new guest stars!

To promote the original *Speak Now*, Taylor sang on a tour bus round Hollywood!

NEW ADDITION

In the early days of The Eras Tour, **'Enchanted'** was the **only track from *Speak Now* to feature in the main set**. That changed after the *Taylor's Version* album was released in July 2023, as fans got to sing and dance along with **'Long Live'** for the rest of 2023, too!

SET IN STONE

Vault track **'When Emma Falls In Love'** is one of the most obsessed-over tracks in T-Swift's catalogue. That's because **fans reckon it's written about Taylor's close friend, the actress Emma Stone**. Tay has neither confirmed nor denied the rumour!

A TAYLOR FAVOURITE

"I love this album because it **tells a tale of growing up, flailing, flying and crashing** ... and living to speak about it," Taylor said in an Instagram post to tie in with the announcement of *Speak Now (TV)*.

NOT SO FOOLISH

The original *Speak Now* album was **written by Swift on her own**, to prove to the world that she didn't need outside help to pen a smash hit. She stayed true to that approach with all the new Vault tracks, such as **'Foolish One'** and **'Electric Touch'** featuring **Fall Out Boy**!

RETURN OF THE KING

Taylor flipped things back to the future with the video for **'I Can See You'**. Celebs **Joey King** and **Presley Cash** appeared in the vid for **'Mean'** when it was originally released in 2011. So Tay brought them both back, alongside **Taylor Lautner**, for the new album's first single!

SORRY, MILEY

As usual, records tumbled with the release of *Speak Now (Taylor's Version)*. **Tay overtook Barbra Streisand's record** for the most number 1 albums by a female artist ever, with 12 in total. This was also Taylor's **fifth year in a row with a number 1 album**, surpassing **Miley Cyrus**!

FOREVER ENCHANTED

In a Reddit vote, **'Enchanted'** and **'Long Live'** shared the honour of **fans' favourite song** from *Speak Now (Taylor's Version)*, with tearful **'Back To December'** finishing third. Sadly, **'Superman'** came in last. Fans from 44 different countries voted!

Taylor certainly looked enchanting as *Speak Now* won Top Country Album at the Billboard Music Awards in 2011.

TOTALLY TAYLOR: BEST DRESSED TOUR GOERS

Swifties never go out of style – as these devoted fans proved when they showed up to The Eras Tour!

MISS AMERICANA ...

... and the **Heartbreak Prince**! Yep, this pair dressed up to match the **opening track of The Eras Tour** set during its final 3-show run in Vancouver. Awesome!

Kudos to this pair for taking the opening song literally!

BRACELET CRAZINESS

Thanks to one line from **'You're On Your Own, Kid'**, swapping **friendship bracelets** became the top priority as soon as you arrived! These Canadian fans in Toronto came very well prepared.

Emma's idea was popular with other fans at Wembley!

THE SMALLEST MEN

A fan from New York called Emma had an ingenious style idea when she attended a London show. She based her dress on **'The Smallest Man Who Ever Lived'**, inviting other fans to **write the names of their exes** on it!

Fans put so much thought into their concert outfits!

ERA VS ERA

One of the toughest choices to make before attending a show was **which Era to represent**! These 3 London fans faced off as ***Lover* vs *Taylor Swift* vs *The Tortured Poets Department***. You decide who won!

MAYOR MAGIC

Even **Toronto's mayor** made sure to look the part when Taylor came to town! Olivia Chow showed up to a fan event before the big show in a ***Speak Now* themed dress** and **cowboy boots**. Cool!

Olivia Chow must go down as the coolest mayor in Canada!

HAPPY SNAPS

It wasn't all about swish dresses! These 2 Wembley fans instead went for fancy dress to celebrate **Tay's love of Polaroid cameras** … or is it a **'Picture To Burn'**?

Which emoji would you have worn to The Eras Tour?!

All glammed up and ready to sing at the top of their lungs all night!

COWBOY HATS

Another massive **Eras Tour trend** was completing your outfit with a cowboy hat – bonus points for **sparkles**! It was a brilliant nod to Taylor's **country music** origins. These 2 Wembley fans are justifiably pleased with their work!

13 ... BEST TAYLOR EASTER EGGS

Taylor has snuck secret messages into her music and videos from day one! These are just a few you may have missed ...

1 THE LOVER SIGN

When Taylor released the video for **'ME!'**, featuring Brendon Urie, her fanbase went into a frenzy trying to figure out what her **upcoming seventh album** would be called. The eagle-eyed spotted the **bright pink *Lover* sign** on top of a distant building.

Fans know about Taylor's 13 obsession, and often write it on their hands at gigs!

2 ALL THE 13S

TayTay naturally does her best to slip her **favourite number** into as many places as possible. A clock in **'cardigan'** has its hands on the 1 and the 3, there's a piece of 13 graffiti in **'...Ready For It?'** and the intro to **'Call It What You Want'** lasts precisely 13 seconds!

3 SAYONARA, SNAKE

A **vengeful snake** has become so synonymous with Taylor and the *Reputation* era, that you might have missed her **saying goodbye** to it in **'You Need To Calm Down'**! A back tattoo shows a **snake morphing into an explosion of butterflies**, to usher in the *Lover* era.

4 SPEAK NOW TV

The **'Bejeweled'** video is legendary for all its teases towards ***Speak Now (Taylor's Version)***. The lift contains a purple button containing the **number 13**, Laura Dern utters the words **"Speak not"** and Tay recreates a legendary **balcony moment** from the original *Speak Now* tour!

5 THE TORTURED GRAMMYS DEPARTMENT

Taylor snuck in Easter eggs for 2 different projects at the **2024 Grammys**. Her black-and-white dress teased **'The Albatross'** from upcoming record *The Tortured Poets Department*. Meanwhile her choker was a **watch set to midnight** – you can figure out what that was a reference to!

6 THE BLUE DRESS

The blue dress from the **'Out Of The Woods'** video is said to be the same one Taylor wore while **splitting up** with Harry Styles – confirming the song is about him. Amazingly, it's the same dress she went on to reference in **'Is It Over Now?'**, 9 years later!

Joe Alwyn is an actor who has appeared in *The Brutalist*, *The Favourite* and *Mary Queen Of Scots*.

7

WILLIAM BOWERY

A **mysterious new songwriter** collaborated with Taylor on *folklore* tracks **'exile'** and **'betty'**. Fans eventually twigged it was then-beau **Joe Alwyn**. His grandfather is called William, and the pair stayed at NYC's Bowery Hotel in their early days as a couple!

8

TRIBUTE TO GRANDMA

The beautiful song **'marjorie'**, from *evermore*, is all about Taylor's relationship with her grandma. Marjorie Finlay was an **opera singer**, and at the end of the song you can hear an operatic voice **singing in the background**. That really is her!

9

NO SCOOTERS

T-Swift's path to releasing the *Taylor's Version* albums started after she **fell out with her old boss**, a man named Scooter Braun. He's referenced in the video to **'The Man'**, with a sign that reads 'No Scooters'!

10

THE BETTY LOVE TRIANGLE

One of the most important themes on *folklore* is the **love triangle** between James, Inez and Betty. While the characters are fictional, they're actually named after 3 real people – **Blake Lively and Ryan Reynolds' children**!

11

LABYRINTH OF WORDS

Taylor received an **honorary degree** from NYU in 2022. Her acceptance speech was hugely inspiring – but she also **snuck in some secret lyrics**! "Breathe in, breath through, breathe deep, breathe out," turned out to be from *Midnights* track **'Labyrinth'**.

Taylor was clearly ecstatic to receiver her honorary degree from New York University!

12

THE ERAS TOUR

Can a tour feature Easter eggs? Fans reckon so, particularly when you look at the **opening song choices**. Most agree that Taylor kicked off with the ***Lover* era** because it would have been her previous tour – but it was sadly cancelled due to the pandemic.

13

NOT A LOT ...

Her most famous Easter egg is the phrase **"not a lot going on at the moment."** It usually means she's about to release new music! She used the famous slogan from the **'22' T-shirt** before both *folklore* and *evermore*. Let's hope to see it again in 2025!

SWIFTIES' ACTIVITIES

ERAS TOUR WORDSEARCH

Taylor's favourite number is 13 ... so can you find all 13 favourites from The Eras Tour?

A	D	G	O	I	G	K	N	S	T	K	P	R	S
D	M	N	M	C	V	F	E	A	R	L	E	S	S
X	W	A	R	E	A	D	Y	F	O	R	I	T	F
T	S	L	S	J	Z	P	M	W	Y	M	W	V	B
H	P	O	K	T	V	B	R	T	I	P	Q	A	E
E	B	V	A	B	E	X	L	O	W	L	C	K	T
M	A	E	R	A	U	R	N	E	B	N	L	M	T
A	D	R	M	W	S	D	M	F	K	O	S	O	Y
N	B	A	A	Q	H	I	M	I	B	P	T	J	W
W	L	K	A	U	G	U	S	T	N	C	Y	B	Y
N	O	A	R	I	N	H	L	F	O	D	L	M	G
R	O	G	F	H	S	J	K	A	M	C	E	L	P
A	D	M	P	D	E	N	C	H	A	N	T	E	D
D	E	L	I	C	A	T	E	B	S	E	I	O	Z

AUGUST
BAD BLOOD
BETTY
DELICATE
ENCHANTED
FEARLESS
KARMA
LOVER
THE MAN
MASTERMIND
READY FOR IT
STYLE
WILLOW

SWIFTIES' ACTIVITIES

100% UNOFFICIAL

MAKE THE FRIENDSHIP BRACELETS

Fill in the gaps to make a friendship bracelet from each Era! It could be an album name or song title.

1 R S N G

2 S H A E T F F

3 L O L V E

4 E E R M R E

5 L V E S O Y

6 N D G M

7 C R L S M M E R

8 S L T R

9 P A K S F L

10 A T I E R

11 F L R I D

1989 (TAYLOR'S VERSION)

BACK IN STYLE

Taylor announced *1989 (TV)* during her final Eras Tour show in LA – and it came out just 2 months later! It's named after Tay's year of birth, and it's the poppiest record of her career. The original version, back in 2014, featured 3 number 1s: 'Shake It Off', 'Blank Space' and 'Bad Blood'.

1989 was a huge fan favourite even before 'Is It Over Now?'!

FLASHING LIGHTS

Taylor doesn't have to do much to go viral, and sure enough Vault track **'Is It Over Now?'** became a TikTok phenomenon. **Fans created their own dance** to the ridiculously catchy bridge which was copied around the world. One fan even recorded herself performing it before **bungee jumping** off Auckland Harbour!

1989 ICON

Famous songwriter **Diane Warren** co-wrote Vault track **'Say Don't Go'**. Her huge hits include **'I Don't Want To Miss A Thing'** by noisy rockers Aerosmith. Diane didn't hear the finished version of **'Say Don't Go'** until 2 hours before it was released!

SHORT AND SWEET

New Vault track **'Now That We Don't Talk'** is the **shortest song** on the album, at just 2 minutes and 26 seconds. That's still enough time for Tay to express relief that she no longer has to like her **ex's music taste** and love of expensive yachts! Most fans believe it's about splitting up with Harry Styles.

SWEDISH DELICACY

Fan fave **'Style'** came about in a unique way. Its unforgettable intro hook was an instrumental piece that **guitarist Niklas Ljungfelt** played to **producer Max Martin**. Taylor overheard it, loved it, and one of her most beloved tracks was born!

SPECIAL EDITIONS

1989 (Taylor's Version) was a **collector's dream** – or maybe a collector's nightmare! There were **14 different editions** released: 5 uniquely coloured vinyls, 8 on CD and an old-school cassette, too. The deluxe edition of the album featured a remix of **'Bad Blood'**, starring Kendrick Lamar.

TAYLOR T-TIME

"This moment is a reflection of **the woods** we've wandered **through** and all **this love** between us still glowing in **the darkest dark**," Taylor wrote in the prologue to the album. Can you recognise any *1989* **lyrics** Taylor cleverly snuck into her words?

Annie Lennox sang in the 1980s band Eurythmics.

OLD ROMANTICS

Taylor was heavily **inspired by the music of the 1980s** in writing the original record – hence naming it after her birth year! It's full of synthesisers, drum pads and toe-tapping beats. **Annie Lennox** and **Peter Gabriel** were 2 of her biggest influences.

Taylor promoted the original *1989* album by performing at the very trendy Victoria's Secret Fashion Show. Amazing!

13 ... TOP ERAS TOUR SUPPORT ACTS

Taylor had support from plenty of artists on her Eras Tour dates. These were the most memorable ...

1 GAYLE

Amazingly, the very first performer on The Eras Tour wasn't Taylor – well, at least not Taylor Swift! Instead, the honour went to this **Texas rock chick**, whose biggest hit is called **'ABCDEFU'**. The uncanny part? Her first name is also Taylor!

2 PARAMORE

Hayley Williams' band Paramore shared the honour of opening The Eras Tour in Arizona with Gayle. The band returned the following summer, to belt out hits such as **'Still Into You'** at Wembley Stadium!

3 GRACIE ABRAMS

Super-talented Gracie rocketed to fame on the back of her Eras Tour appearances. She was nominated for **Best New Artist** at the Grammy Awards 2024, and grabbed her first UK number 1 with **'I Love You, I'm Sorry'**.

Gracie Abrams is the daughter of famous filmmaker JJ Abrams. His movies include *Star Wars: The Rise of Skywalker*!

4 PHOEBE BRIDGERS

It's usually Taylor who mops up at awards shows. But at the **2024 Grammy Awards**, it was Phoebe's turn! She won Best Alternative Music Album, Best Rock Song, Best Rock Performance and Best Pop Duo/Group Performance, with SZA.

As well as making 6 ace albums, Sabrina was also the voice of Princess Vivian in *Sofia the First*!

5 SABRINA CARPENTER

Yet another Taylor support act and friend who is now a household name, thanks to tracks like **'Espresso'** and **'Please Please Please'**. Sabrina joined The Eras Tour for dates in South America, Australia and Singapore.

6 HAIM

Taylor and the coolest girl group around go way back. They appeared together in the music video for **'Bejeweled'** and recorded the awesome **'no body, no crime'** for *evermore*. In California, Haim opened for Taylor, then later returned to duet on that hit!

7 RAYE

Raye joined Taylor for one night in London, but incredibly that may not have been her ultimate highlight of 2024. Instead, it was surely the **Brit Awards**, where she claimed 6 shiny trophies – the most ever by a single artist!

8 MUNA

These **veteran rockers** have been around since 2013, and know exactly how to **warm up a crowd**. Before linking up with Taylor, they'd also supported Harry Styles, Kacey Musgraves, Lorde and Phoebe Bridgers!

9 MAISIE PETERS

Second album ***The Good Witch*** saw Maisie became the youngest female solo artist to have a **UK number 1** in 10 years. Things got even better the following summer, when she was invited to join Taylor for night 7 at Wembley!

10 GIRL IN RED

Norway's latest export became popular by writing **songs about mental health** in her bedroom. She still lives in her home country, but crossed the pond to join Taylor for dates in Chicago, Detroit and Pittsburgh.

Beabadoobee was born in the Philippines and moved to the UK when she was 3!

11 BEABADOOBEE

Filipino-British up-and-comer Beabadoobee was a regular on The Eras Tour in its early days across America. She gained even more success a year later, as third album ***This Is How Tomorrow Moves*** reached **number 1** in the UK!

12 LOUTA

Taylor drafted in a local favourite for her 3 Eras Tour gigs in **Argentina**. Louta is a DJ, producer and songwriter from Buenos Aires, whose hits include the endlessly toe-tapping **'Tau Tau'**.

13 HOLLY HUMBERSTONE

This Grantham girl lists **Phoebe Bridgers** and **Haim** as 2 of her biggest career influences, and says she is inspired by "female writers who overshare". Little wonder she fit right in opening for Taylor on night 5 at **Wembley**!

TOTALLY TAYLOR: ERAS TOUR FAN FRENZY

It wasn't just Tay and her crew who got swept up in The Eras Tour. Her fans, and in some cases entire cities, were feeling the love, too!

BRAZIL GOES BONKERS

The 125-foot **Christ The Redeemer** statue above **Rio de Janiero** is one of Brazil's biggest landmarks. To greet Taylor, the sanctuary in charge did something special. They **illuminated the statue** to look like it was wearing a T-shirt with **'Welcome to Brazil'** on it, inspired by the **'Junior Jules'** T-shirt from **'You Belong With Me'**!

Brazil's most famous landmark was redecorated just for Taylor!

SWIFTCOUVER TAKEOVER

The giant **Vancouver sign** along the city's waterfront is among its most memorable places. So when Taylor came to town, **13 more sprang up** in the same style, featuring Taylor song titles! **'Down Bad'**, **'willow'**, **'Lover'** and **'Delicate'** were just some of the signs Swifties found, and posed in front of.

Vancouver was the very final stop on The Eras Tour. Awww!

Everyone agreed the silent disco carriage was a Toronto highlight!

WEMBLEY WONDERS

With **8 dates in London**, the UK's capital city was always going over the top for T-Swift. Sure enough, the **Wembley Park gallery put on a free photo exhibition**, while local group **City String Ensemble** played classic versions of her biggest hits – again for free. Even famous restaurant Gaucho got in on the act, offering a **Taylor-themed brunch**!

Wembley went all in for Taylor's visits in summer 2024.

TORONTO TRIUMPH

Vancouver wasn't the only Canadian city to go **Taylor crazy**. In Toronto, the local convention centre hosted an awesome event called **Taylgate '24**. Fans could make **friendship bracelets**, enter **fancy dress competitions**, and leap aboard a converted subway train covered in hearts for a **silent Swifties' disco**!

THE ERAS TOUR WEDDING

Astonishingly, one loved-up couple **got married during an Eras Tour gig**! René Hurtado and Max Bochman exchanged their vows during a break in TayTay's set in Glendale, Arizona. Naturally they wore a **white dress and tuxedo** for the occasion!

CELEBRITY HILARITY

An internet meme proved that even celebrities lose their minds over Taylor. A widely circulated video showed actors **Phoebe Waller-Bridge** and **Andrew Scott** leaving the VIP tent, presumably to get a drink – only to sprint back as fast as possible when the opening chords to **'Style'** kicked in!

Phoebe Waller-Bridge and Andrew Scott, staying in style!

SWIFTIES' ACTIVITIES

WHICH TAYLOR ERA ARE YOU?

Whether you attended The Eras Tour or just love listening to Taylor at home, everyone has an era they relate to the most. Take this quiz to find out which era you are!

1 Which of these colours best suits your personality?

A – Gold
B – Purple
C – Green
D – Black

2 What's your preferred music genre?

A – Country
B – Pop
C – Acoustic
D – Rock

3 What type of movies do you most enjoy watching?

A – Cheery rom-coms
B – Disney classics
C – Gentle documentaries
D – Moody thrillers

4 Which artist's music are you most likely to listen to?

A – Maren Morris
B – Paramore
C – Bon Iver
D – Future

5 Which footwear do you prefer to wear?

A – Chunky trainers
B – High heels
C – Sandals
D – Big boots

6 Which of these animals would you most like as a pet?

A – Horse
B – Firefly
C – Wolf
D – Snake

7 Which of these Taylor tracks do you know best?

A – 'Hey Stephen'
B – 'Dear John'
C – 'marjorie'
D – 'King Of My Heart'

Would you rock this outfit, or pick comfy, chunky trainers?

Now tally up your answers and put the number in each box!

A ☐ B ☐ C ☐ D ☐

Which letter did you score most on? That one reveals your Taylor Era ...

A You are *Fearless*!

Taylor's pop hits still get your toes tapping, but it's the classic country tunes that you love most. **'Love Story'** and **'You Belong To Me'** are the first songs on any custom playlist, and every outfit has to be finished off with just a little bit of gold!

B You are *Speak Now*!

You love a purple dress and go to bed at night dreaming of being transported from your bedroom to a sparkling Disney castle. You know every word to **'Enchanted'** and desperately hope Taylor plays **'Sparks Fly'** on her next tour!

C You are *evermore*!

While your mates are planning their next big night out, you prefer the idea of wrapping up in a **'cardigan'**, putting your feet up and keeping things cosy. You dress for comfort – but still look great – and love a Taylor acoustic set!

D You are *Reputation*!

You live life with a cheeky glint in your eye and aren't afraid of what people think of you. Taylor's rockier tracks like **'...Ready For It?'** are your faves – and your ultimate birthday gift would be the one-legged black-and-red (or gold) bodysuit she wore on The Eras Tour!

ALBUM SPOTLIGHT

TAYLOR SWIFT HOLIDAY COLLECTION

MERRY SWIFTMAS

Did you know that TayTay has her own Christmas album? It's not an official part of her albums timeline and only contains 6 tracks. But most fans still consider it essential holiday listening. Just don't ever expect a *Taylor's Version* of this one!

Tay's festive album came out when she was just 17!

WINTER WONDERLAND

Taylor Swift Holiday Collection came out in October 2007, containing **6 tracks**. 4 of its songs are cover versions, meaning they were originally performed by other artists. 2 are her own tracks: **'Christmases When You Were Mine'** and **'Christmas Must Be Something More'**.

LONG WAIT

British fans will recognise **'Last Christmas'** as one of the most well-known festive hits. It was originally **released by Wham in 1984**. Yet, it was another 37 years before George Michael and Andrew Ridgeley's catchy tune finally reached number 1, in 2021!

PERSONAL APPEARANCE

Swifties based in **New York** got a special treat when she launched the album with an **autograph signing at NBC's Experience Store**. She's way too famous to do something like that now! Taylor also performed **'Silent Night'** at the nearby Rockefeller Center, on a super-cool rhinestoned guitar!

SPRING SEQUEL

Taylor Swift Holiday Collection was followed up by another **mini-album called *Beautiful Eyes***. It was only released in Walmart stores, across the USA. Tracks included an acoustic version of **'Teardrops On My Guitar'** and 2 new songs: **'Beautiful Eyes'** and **'I Heart ?'**.

CHURCH CLASSIC

Festive favourite **'Silent Night'** is not only the oldest song on the album, but also the oldest that Taylor has ever recorded! The **Christmas carol** was written in **Germany** in 1818, and originally called 'Stille Nacht, heilige Nacht'. It's also been covered by **Mariah Carey**!

LEPPARD SPOTS

This was a **creative era** for Taylor, in terms of **building her fame and credibility**. A few months after her Christmas record, she filmed a special gig with massive '80s rock band **Def Leppard**. It's called *CMT Crossroads* and their versions of **'Picture To Burn'** and **'When Love & Hate Collide'** are fantastic!

FARM GIRL

12 years after her Christmas album, Taylor released a seasonal single. **'Christmas Tree Farm'** was inspired by her growing up on – you've guessed it! – a **Christmas tree farm in Wyomissing, Pennsylvania**. She wrote, recorded and released the tune in under 6 days!

Taylor loves Christmas so much! She performed at Capital's Jingle Bell Ball in December 2019, where she debuted 'Christmas Tree Farm' live.

TOTALLY TAYLOR: FAMOUS SWIFTIES

The Eras Tour wasn't just about the music, the fans and the support acts. Celebs were all over it too! Here's how they celebrated their favourite musician ...

JEDWARD

The Irish double act got ready for it ahead of Taylor's **Dublin** show by John singing, um, **'...Ready For It?'** on TikTok. They went one better during the gig itself, belting out **'Enchanted'** with Taylor performing behind them. They **met fans** outside Wembley when Tay came to **London**, too!

Jedward ready to swap friendship bracelets outside Wembley!

ALYSON HANNIGAN

The *Buffy the Vampire Slayer* actress **attended multiple nights** of The Eras Tour – including the very last one, in **Vancouver**! "It was **beyond epic** in every way," she wrote on Instagram. "Thanks everyone involved for bringing **true magic** into our world and forever in my heart and soul."

Alyson Hannigan is one of the most committed celebrity Swifties!

PRINCE WILLIAM

Prince William took both his son Prince George and daughter Princess Charlotte to **Wembley** to see Taylor – and was famously **captured in a selfie** with her backstage! It's scored over **3.1 million likes** on Instagram.

Prince William shared a selfie with Taylor on his personal Instagram!

Tay once gave Channing Tatum some home-made pop tarts!

CHANNING TATUM

The star of *Magic Mike* took his daughter Everly to see Taylor in **Los Angeles** and even sported a **custom T-shirt** especially for the occasion. It read **"it's me, hi, I'm the dad, it's me"** in honour of **'Anti-Hero'**!

Taylor and Gigi first met at the 2014 Vanity Fair Oscar Party.

SARAH MICHELLE GELLAR

The queen of *Buffy The Vampire Slayer* took daughter Charlotte along to see Taylor in **Los Angeles**, where she met up with all-sister group **Haim** and **Seth Green**, who played Oz in the classic vamp-killing show!

Sarah took a day off work to go watch The Eras Tour!

GIGI HADID

Taylor's modelling mate was one of many famous faces in the **'Bad Blood'** video, so it was only natural that she'd also pop up on The Eras Tour. She attended the **Nashville** show and a fan video also caught her **singing along to 'Cruel Summer'** in Santa Clara!

HUGH GRANT

"Dear @taylorswift13," Grant wrote on X after seeing Taylor at **Wembley**, "You have an incredible show, an amazing and v hospitable team and excellent if gigantic boyfriend. Thanks so much from one ageing **London boy**, wife and thrilled 8 year old #halfgirlhalfbracelet." He's clearly a huge fan!

Hugh said his daughter and her friend were "bopping away" throughout!

13 ... BEST MUSIC VIDEOS

Some feature celebs, others have seen her totally restyle herself – these are the best vids of TayTay's career!

1

DELICATE

To quote another song off ***Reputation*** – this one is just gorgeous! Tay toe-taps her way though a **packed hotel lobby** and **underground station**, before **going barefoot in a rainy street** – a **dance routine** that's just as delicate as the song itself.

Tay shows off delicate moves in the video to, um, 'Delicate'!

2

BAD BLOOD

The **most famous** vid of Taylor's career, simply for the **number of famous names** involved. Among them are **Ellie Goulding, Lena Dunham, Gigi Hadid, Cara Delevingne,** and **Cindy Crawford!**

3

BEJEWELED

Superstar **sister squad Haim** have crossed paths with Tay numerous times and do so in hilarious fashion in the **'Bejeweled'** vid. They play her **evil stepsisters**, but Taylor has the last laugh. It's bad news for **Jack Antonoff** though – he gets ghosted after proposing!

4

WILDEST DREAMS

This ***1989*** favourite sees Taylor sport **jet-black hair** on the set of a **pretend movie filmed in South Africa and Botswana**. *Wrath of Man* actor **Scott Eastwood** plays Taylor's fictional co-star and love interest Robert Kingsley.

'Wildest Dreams' brought a very cool change of hair colour.

5

ALL TOO WELL: THE SHORT FILM

This **15-minute** classic written and directed by Taylor herself sees **Sadie Sink** from *Stranger Things* and *Teen Wolf* star **Dylan O'Brien** bring the *Red* smash hit to life in **utterly heartbreaking** fashion. You're only allowed to cry once! OK, twice.

6 LOVE STORY

It may be from her second album, but this is considered Taylor's **breakthrough video**. The **Romeo and Juliet** story saw Taylor look stunning in a medieval corset and was filmed at **Castle Gwynn in Tennessee**.

7 THE MAN

Who plays the **dude swaggering around the office** and throwing a strop on the tennis court in this clip? **Ummm, it's Taylor Swift!** It took Tay up to **6 hours in the make-up chair** for each shoot – and she **directed the whole thing**, too!

8 LOOK WHAT YOU MADE ME DO

Zombie Taylor! **Diamonds** in the bath Taylor! **Snake Queen** Taylor! For the most epic comeback single of her career, T-Swift took on multiple guises – and The Eras Tour has cemented this song as **one of her most unforgettable**.

Yes, this really is Taylor! Under all that facial hair and clothing!

9 BLANK SPACE

Super big-budget video in which Taylor appears to have **the life of anyone's dreams**, with a **handsome husband** and **opulent mansion**. But, oh, what fun she clearly has **tearing it all to pieces**, after discovering her guy has texted another girl!

10 FORTNIGHT

Everything went **black and white** for the debut single from *The Tortured Poets Department*, in which Tay and guest star **Post Malone** duel it out on **typewriters**. As for the outro, with Tay **singing in the pouring rain** ... phenomenal!

11 YOU NEED TO CALM DOWN

This one is all about the **celebrity cameos**. The cast of **Queer Eye** pop in for tea and **Adam Lambert** tattoos **Ellen DeGeneres**. Best of all, **Katy Perry** – who was rivals with TayTay for years – turns up for a make-up hug. The pair are dressed as a **burger and fries**!

12 SHAKE IT OFF

With **3.6 billion views** and 13 million likes, this is the **most popular video** of Taylor's career. Again, it's one in which she adopts numerous guises, including **Ballet Taylor, Casual Taylor and Cheerleader Taylor.** Cool!

You'll have to watch this one a million times to spot all the Easter eggs!

13 I CAN DO IT WITH A BROKEN HEART

Sad **The Eras Tour** is over? Then spend an hour of your life watching this on repeat! It contains loads of **backstage Easter eggs**, fans going wild, rehearsal clips and other magic moments. The best tribute to the **best tour ever!**

THE ULTIMATE SWIFTIES' TRIVIA QUIZ

How closely have you been paying attention to this book? Find out with these TayTay brainteasers – all covering topics from previous pages ...

1 What is Taylor's star sign?
A. Capricorn
B. Scorpio
C. Sagittarius

2 Which of these songs was Taylor's first ever single?
A. 'Teardrops On My Guitar'
B. 'Tim McGraw'
C. 'Love Story'

How well do you know Taylor's very first album?

3 Which city hosted the most dates on The Eras Tour?
A. London
B. Los Angeles
C. Toronto

4 Which album was the first to get a Taylor's Version?
A. *Fearless*
B. *Red*
C. *1989*

Tay and Ed go way back, but which song did they sing together?

5 Which Ed Sheeran and Taylor track did the pair play at Wembley?
A. 'Shivers'
B. 'Perfect'
C. 'Everything Has Changed'

6 **How many times has Taylor won the Grammy for Album of the Year?**

A. 3
B. 4
C. 5

TayTay has literally won armfuls of Grammys!

The start of The Eras Tour. But which song did she play?

7 **What was the opening song on The Eras Tour?**

A. 'Miss Americana & The Heart-Break Prince'
B. 'Cruel Summer'
C. 'The Man'

8 **Which era is all about the colour purple?**

A. *Speak Now*
B. *Midnights*
C. *The Tortured Poets Department*

9 **How many days did it take Taylor to write, record and release 'Christmas Tree Farm'?**

A. 3
B. 6
C. 9

10 **Which Taylor collaborator gets ghosted in the video to 'Bejeweled'?**

A. Brendon Urie
B. Aaron Dessner
C. Jack Antonoff

How did you do?

0–3:
Don't be down bad. Keep reading this book nightly and you'll be a TayTay expert in no time!

4–6:
You've definitely been paying attention. Now see if you can go back and spot the answers you missed!

7–9:
An enchanted performance, and so close to perfection. You definitely know your T-Swift!

10:
Time to go dancing – like you're made of starlight! Consider yourself a Taylor trivia king or queen.

ALBUM SPOTLIGHT

TS12

WHAT'S NEXT FOR TAYTAY?

Taylor Swift's next record is one of the most anticipated in music history. You can bet the most famous artist on the planet will reinvent herself yet again for the follow-up to *The Tortured Poets Department* – and that it will smash records. Are you ready for it? Duh ... yeah!

Fans suspect that orange will be the theme of TS12!

ROLL ON 2026

Taylor traditionally **releases an album every 2 years**. She changed that schedule for *Reputation*, taking an extra year out of the spotlight, and *folklore* and *evermore* – but that's because everyone was in lockdown. Assuming she's back on her usual timeline, you can expect to hear *TS12* in **2026**!

PAINT THE TOWN ORANGE

Taylor usually **chooses a colour** to match each era and album. *Speak Now* was purple, *Reputation* was black and *Red* speaks for itself. With 11 albums, she's covered most of the biggies, but fans point out that one omission stands out: **maybe the theme of *TS12* will be orange!**

FAMILIAR FACES ...

Jack Antonoff and Aaron Dessner are expected to be the main **producers of *TS12***. They've been Taylor's go-to guys **since *folklore***, and split duties on *The Tortured Poets Department*. Most of the main album tracks were made with Antonoff, while Dessner largely focussed on the extra songs for *The Anthology*.

BIG BOOK TEASE

One line from the official Eras Tour Book has fuelled **speculation** about what's next. In the intro, Taylor writes **"See you next era"**. *TS12* could take Tay into **unexplored territory** – pop beats and big choruses, perhaps?

ALL ABOUT TRAVIS

Relationships are a major theme of every Taylor record, from the **romance** of *Lover* to the **heartbreak** of *The Tortured Poets Department*. But 2 positive songs from that last album, **'So High School'** and **'The Alchemy'**, touched on her budding relationship with Travis Kelce. Assuming they stay together, **expect more anthems in that vein on *TS12*!**

NECKLACE MYSTERY

One **possible Easter egg** for the album materialised in September 2024. Taylor stepped out for dinner with Gigi Hadid, wearing a **gold necklace that appeared to have a 12 in the middle**. Some fans speculated that it was a sign that *TS12* was already underway – however, others pointed out it could have simply been her initials, TS, flipped upside down!

... AND SURPRISE ADDITIONS

TS12 will surely **feature a collab**! **Haim** and **Ed Sheeran** are among those you'd expect to work with Taylor again. Maybe **Gracie Abrams, Sabrina Carpenter** and **Phoebe Bridgers**, who found global fame during the tour?

Taylor looked more confident than ever to kick off 2025 at the Grammy Awards. You can bet *TS12* is going to be phenomenal!

13 ... VAULT TRACKS YOU NEED TO HEAR RIGHT NOW

The astonishing thing about the *Taylor's Versions* is the selection of additional Vault tracks! Here are some of the best ...

1 IS IT OVER NOW?

A glorious addition to *1989 (Taylor's Version)*, which spawned **endless TikTok memes** and became Taylor's **11th number 1 single** in her home country. In Buenos Aires, she blended it with **'Out Of The Woods'** for a spectacular surprise song!

2 ALL TOO WELL (10 MINUTE VERSION)

When *Red* was released, Taylor said **'All Too Well'** "started out probably being a 10-minute song, which you **can't put in an album**". 9 years later, after **fans clamoured** on a daily basis, she finally did exactly that!

3 TIMELESS

T-Swift is a **compelling storyteller** and in this *Speak Now (Taylor's Version)* number, she **dips into history** while exploring an **antiques store**. Among the references are a **soldier** heading off to war and teenagers going to a **dance** – in 1958!

4 RUN

The first song Taylor ever penned with **Ed Sheeran** was written on **the day they met**! However, we had to wait nearly a decade to hear it, as **'Everything Has Changed'** was chosen for the original *Red* instead of **'Run'**.

5 WHEN EMMA FALLS IN LOVE

This *Speak Now (TV)* track isn't only intriguing because it's (apparently!) about Tay's friend **Emma Stone**. It also features guest appearances from cool indie musicians. **Beirut's Benjamin Lanz** plays synths, alongside drums by **Big Thief's James Krivchenia**!

6 ELECTRIC TOUCH

Taylor penned *Speak Now* alone, to showcase her **songwriting skills**. Among her influences were emo-rock bands like **Fall Out Boy** – so, when it came to making the *Taylor's Version*, she brought them aboard to **guest on this banger**!

Fall Out Boy have been unleashing emo hits since 2001!

7 SUBURBAN LEGENDS

Another *1989 (Taylor's Version)* addition, in which the narrator is so hooked on her partner that they're willing to **overlook bad behaviour**. Its poppy, **toe-tapping** production fits in perfectly alongside the **'80s-themed beats** of the original album.

Maren Morris has also collaborated with Grey and Zedd.

8 YOU ALL OVER ME

Taylor's **country roots** really are all over this heartbreaker from *Fearless (Taylor's Version)*. **Maren Morris** guests on vocals as Tay reflects on all the **little things that remind her of an ex**, like the day in June on which they first met.

9 THAT'S WHEN

Country icon **Keith Urban** guests on both this and **'We Were Happy'**, from *Fearless (Taylor's Version)*. He was out and about when **Taylor texted him** – so had to listen to the demos in a food court, at a shopping centre!

Taylor performed with both Keith Urban and Tim McGraw in 2013!

10 SAY DON'T GO

The Vault tracks from *1989 (Taylor's Version)* border on faultless, and **'Say Don't Go'** is another masterclass in **post-breakup sadness**. Tay demoed it on New Year's Day 2014 – but **it was 9 years before it was finished**!

11 THE VERY FIRST NIGHT

This bop from *Red (Taylor's Version)* is fascinating because it sounds like a **tease for her next record, *1989***. It's about reminiscing on a **past relationship**, including a message written on a **polaroid** – and a kitchen **dance party**!

12 NOW THAT WE DON'T TALK

Taylor describes this as "one of my **favourite songs** that was left behind" from the original *1989* sessions – and it's a **disco-pop classic**, despite being less than 3 minutes long. No more acid rock for TayTay!

13 BYE BYE BABY

No one does heartbreak like Taylor, and it's a familiar tale in this *Fearless (Taylor's Version)* extra. The main character **drives away from a once-steady relationship** in a song with subtle touches – like **out-of-tune piano notes** that signify the saddest end!

TOTALLY TAYLOR: ERAS TOUR STATS

All the stats and numbers from The Eras Tour in one place!

149

The number of Eras Tour shows across 2023 and 2024.

83

Performances of **'The Archer'**, **'the last great american dynasty'** and **'tolerate it'** – before they were cut to make space for *The Tortured Poets Department*!

Tay sang the entire set on a treadmill to get ready for The Eras Tour!

MOST PLAYED SURPRISE SONGS

6: 'You're On Your Own, Kid'
5: 'Death By A Thousand Cuts'
5: 'invisible string'
4: 'Maroon'
3: 'Getaway Car'
3: 'Is It Over Now?'

78

Songs that were only played once, including **'New Romantics'**, **'London Boy'** and **'Mean'**!

62

Number of Eras Tour gigs in the USA, more than any other country! The UK came second with 15, while Canada (third) got 9.

MOST PERFORMANCES ALONGSIDE TAY

12: Phoebe Bridgers
10: Haim
6: Aaron Dessner
4: Gracie Abrams
4: Florence Welch
3: Ice Spice
2: Jack Antonoff
2: Sabrina Carpenter

$2 BILLION

Amount of money grossed from Eras Tour ticket sales!

1,067

Performances of tracks from *Midnights* – the most of any Taylor album!

20,000

Ticketless fans who showed up in Philadelphia – kicking off the fan tradition of Taylor-gating in the car park!

484

Hours Taylor spent onstage during The Eras Tour. That's the equivalent of more than 20 days!

$960

Price paid on eBay for a VIP box of merchandise from the tour, including tote bag, posters and souvenir ticket!

10.1 MILLION

Fans who attended The Eras Tour live!

CUTE COLOURING

Finish off your annual with some mindful colouring of Taylor's favourite things!

ANSWERS:

P.28 – The Blank Spaces Quiz

1. 'Tim McGraw'
2. Christmas tree
3. *Fearless*
4. December
5. Sadie Sink / Dylan O'Brien
6. *1989*
7. Snake
8. Brendon
9. 'Cruel Summer'
10. Paris
11. 'exile'
12. 'marjorie'
13. Este / Danielle / Alana
14. Lavender
15. London

P.37 – Reputation Snake Maze

P.44 – Eras Tour Wordsearch

P.45 – Make the Friendship Bracelets

P.60 – The Ultimate Swifties' Trivia Quiz

1. C, **2.**B, **3.**A, **4.**A, **5.**C, **6.**B, **7.**A, **8.**A, **9.**B, **10.**C

CREDITS

Front cover: PICTURES: Alamy Images, PA Images
5: PICTURES: Alamy Images, PA Images
6–7: PICTURES: Shutterstock, Tinseltown / Alamy Images, Image Press Agency / Alamy Images, Thomas Jackson / Shutterstock, Brian Friedman
8–9: PICTURES: Alamy Images, Sipa US / Shutterstock, Varvara Krauchanka / Shutterstock, Tinseltown
10–11: WORDS: X, @taylorswift13: Taylor Swift, 2025
PICTURES: Alamy Images, Cal Sport Media / Alamy Images, GTCRFOTO / Shutterstock, Brian Friedman / Thea McDonald, Chloe Smithers and Zoe Diamond / Shutterstock, Christian Bertrand / Shutterstock, Tinseltown
12–13: PICTURES: Shutterstock, Chad Robertson Media / Shutterstock, Skyshark Media / Shutterstock, Graham Drew Photography
14–15: WORDS: Variety.com: Taylor Swift / BBC.co.uk: Lily Bottomley
PICTURES: Shutterstock, Christian Bertrand / Alamy Images, Sipa US
16–17: WORDS: Billboard.com: Taylor Swift, Glendale, Arizona concert, 17th March 2023
PICTURES: Shutterstock, Siamionau Pavel / Shutterstock, s_bukley / Alamy Images, Associated Press
18–19: PICTURES: Alamy Images, The Canadian Press / Shutterstock, kiyo360xr / Alamy Images, Thomas Jackson
20–21: PICTURES: Hannah and Ashley Dunger / Ryan Hammond and Mitch Feetham
22–23: PICTURES: Shutterstock, s_bukley / Shutterstock, Kathy Hutchins / Shutterstock, Everett Collection
24–25: WORDS: News.stv.tv: Sophie Carre / Instagram, @threesquarelv: Three Square Food Bank, 22nd March 2023 / X, @OB_Inc_KC: Operation Breakthrough, 21st December 2024
PICTURES: Alamy Images, WENN Rights Ltd / Shutterstock, glenrichardphoto / Alamy Images, Sipa US / Shutterstock, HASPhotos
26–27: PICTURES: Shutterstock, Ben Houdijk / Shutterstock, Christian Bertrand / Alamy Images, Associated Press
28–29: PICTURES: Shutterstock, Tony Norkus / Shutterstock, Christian Bertrand / Shutterstock, Tinseltown
30–31: WORDS: Instagram, @taylorswift: Taylor Swift, 18th June 2021
PICTURES: Shutterstock, Featureflash Photo Agency / YouTube, Taylor Swift, 'All Too Well: The Short Film' music video / Shutterstock, landmarkmedia
32–33: WORDS: BBC.co.uk: Taylor Swift
PICTURES: Shutterstock, DFree / Shutterstock, s_bukley
34–35: PICTURES: Shutterstock, DFree / Alamy Images, Associated Press / Shutterstock, Featureflash Photo Agency / Alamy Images, UPI / Alamy Images, ZUMA Press, Inc.
36: PICTURES: Alamy Images, Stephen Chung
38–39: WORDS: Instagram, @taylorswift: Taylor Swift, 6th May 2023
PICTURES: Shutterstock, Music4mix / Shutterstock, Tinseltown / Shutterstock, Kathy Hutchins
40–41: PICTURES: Alamy Images, Associated Press / Alamy Images, The Canadian Press / Alamy Images, Guy Corbishley / Emily Johnson / Alamy Images, Shawn Goldberg / Alamy Images, Stephen Chung / Hope O'Malley
42–43: WORDS: Billboard.com: Taylor Swift
PICTURES: Shutterstock, Kaitlynn Robinson / Alamy Images, S. A. M. / Alamy Images, UPI
Page 45: PICTURES: Shutterstock, Eli Unger
46–47: WORDS: Instagram, @taylorswift: Taylor Swift, 27th October 2023
PICTURES: Shutterstock, DFree / Shutterstock, s_bukley / Shutterstock, FashionStock.com
48–49: WORDS: Telegraph.co.uk: Holly Humberstone
PICTURES: Alamy Images, Associated Press / Alamy Images, LFP
50–51: PICTURES: Alamy Images, Associated Press / Shutterstock, AlbertArt / Alamy Images, Shawn Goldberg / Alamy Images, Paul Marriott / Shutterstock, Featureflash Photo Agency
52–53: PICTURES: Shutterstock, Featureflash Photo Agency / Shutterstock, Everett Collection / Alamy Images, Associated Press / Shutterstock, Kathy Hutchins
54–55: PICTURES: Alamy Images, MediaPunch Inc / Alamy Images, PA Images
56–57: WORDS: Instagram, @alysonhannigan: Alyson Hannigan, 9th December 2024 / X, @HackedOffHugh: Hugh Grant, 23rd June 2024 / nme.com: Hugh Grant
PICTURES: Alamy Images, Eleventh Hour Photography / Shutterstock, s_bukley / Shutterstock, Mikolaj Barbanell / Shutterstock, Oscar Gonzalez Fuentes / Shutterstock, FashionStock.com / Shutterstock, Featureflash Photo Agency / Shutterstock, Cristiano Barni
58–59: PICTURES: YouTube, Taylor Swift, 'Delicate' music video, 'Wildest Dreams' music video, 'All Too Well: The Short Film' music video, 'The Man' music video, 'I Can Do It With A Broken Heart' music video
60–61: PICTURES: Alamy Images, Associated Press / Shutterstock, Christian Bertrand / Shutterstock, s_bukley / Alamy Images, Associated Press
62–63: WORDS: Taylor Swift, *The Official Taylor Swift The Eras Tour Book*, 2024
PICTURES: Alamy Images, Australian Associated Press / Alamy Images, UPI
64–65: WORDS: Good Morning America interview, 22nd October 2012: Taylor Swift / music.tumblr.com: Taylor Swift
PICTURES: YouTube, Taylor Swift, 'All Too Well: The Short Film' music video / Shutterstock, Featureflash Photo Agency / Shutterstock, Kobby Dagan / Shutterstock, L Paul Mann / Alamy Images, Associated Press
66–67: PICTURES: Alamy Images, Thomas Jackson / Shutterstock, christinenguyen